BLESSED YOUTH

SURVIVAL GUIDE

SARAH GRIFFITH LUND

Saint Louis, Missouri

An imprint of Christian Board of Publication

ChalicePress.com

Print: 9780827203235
EPUB: 9780827203242
EPDF: 9780827203259
Bundle: 9780827203266
Multipack: 9780827203273

Printed in the United States of America

Dedicated to the loving memory of
Sydney Elise Griffith

February 13, 2004—
November 2, 2020

Dear Faith Leaders, Youth Ministry Leaders, Volunteers, Teachers, Administrators, Community Leaders, Elected Officials, Parents, and Grandparents:

I hope you will share this guidebook with the children and teens in your life. Perhaps you can share it as part of a series of ongoing conversations about mental health before there is a crisis in your community. You don't have to wait until there is a crisis to share this book.

This guidebook contains information to help readers build up their "survival kit" during times when they have energy to do so before disaster hits. Some of the information is for when readers need to use items in their survival kit. It is need-to-know-right-now information. I've also included tools for self-reflection, so readers can clarify for themselves how they feel and be better prepared to communicate to others how they feel. Next is some basic information defining the most common mental health challenges and describing how children and teens can get help to manage them. Finally, there's some advice for when readers feel ready to take the next step: advocating for themselves and others in their school.

As you work with children and teens, I invite you to think about what it means to be "blessed." How do you define being blessed in your faith or family? Do you use this word very often with children and teens? How is the term used within various youth contexts?

I invite you to think about how your faith community, school community, and family approach mental health. How can you work alongside youth as advocates for mental health access and to erase the stigma of mental illness?

For over twenty years, I've led congregations as a pastor, led a national organization as a mental health advocate in faith communities, and authored books to provide resources for mental health education. My passion for mental health comes from lived experiences with mental health challenges in myself and my family. I know how powerful it is to break the silence about mental illness and seek care and support for treatment and recovery. I know the heartache and the hope of living with mental illness.

Mental illness hides right in front of us sometimes. Shame, stigma, and discrimination towards people experiencing mental illness cause many of us to hide our true feelings, keep silent, and struggle alone. There is a lot of fear in admitting to needing help.

In the fall of 2020, my sixteen-year-old niece Sydney died by suicide. We were shocked and heartbroken. One of her friends told me:

> I always thought I knew Syd well, but I would have never guessed she was struggling to the degree she was when she passed. I can only speak for myself in terms of mental health, but I found that as soon as I learned that there is no shame in needing help things got a lot better. I think those struggling would be shocked to know that there are people who want to support them, and they do not always have to rely on self-sufficiency. And I think most people would help by educating themselves on mental health, especially adults. A listening ear is always helpful, and I think if we could all learn to act as one many people would feel less alone. And for those suffering losses I would want to let them know they'd be doing a service allowing themselves to get the support they need. Syd wouldn't have wanted me to let my mental health suffer, so I didn't.

Please don't wait until there is a suicide in your own family, school, or faith community. Do everything that you can now to provide education, resources, and advocacy for mental health for children and teens. By working together in schools and in faith communities, we can help prevent youth suicide.

Take what is useful here and share it with as many children and teens as you can. Also explore and engage with the information that leading mental health organizations provide—organizations such as Mental Health America, National Alliance on Mental Illness, Child Mind Institute, Mental Health First Aid, and The Trevor Project.

Thank you for being a blessing to children and teens. Thank you for sharing hope and healing.

With gratitude,

Sarah

Dear Blessed Youth,

It's ok not to be ok.

Tell an adult that you are not ok.

It's not your fault that you're not ok.

It gets better.

There is help.

You are loved.

You are not alone.

Your life matters.

I care about you.

Stay.

Love and blessings,

Sarah

P.S. *No matter what, you are loved!*

This guide will give you tools to survive when you are feeling or thinking

- disconnected and confused
- lost and alone
- no one else is feeling what I'm feeling
- no one is there for me
- what is wrong with me?—because no one else seems to feel this way
- there's something different about me
- my life sucks
- I hate myself
- I suck
- I'm stupid
- I'm a disappointment
- everyone hates me
- my life has no meaning
- I don't know how to get help
- I can't do this anymore
- I don't want my life to be like this
- I know people who want to die but I don't know how to help them
- I don't know what's happening to me, but I need help
- I'm not ok

Whatever it is you are feeling is valid. And if you are not struggling right now, remember that it's likely a friend, family member, or someone you love *is* feeling some of these things and *is* struggling. Or maybe you have felt this way in the past or might feel this way in the future. Taking time now to learn more about mental health while you are in a good space will help you in the future.

My Story About Mental Health

I am writing this book because it is the book my family needs. It is the book that I needed as a youth when I felt depressed, anxious, and had thoughts of self-harm. It is the book inspired by my sixteen-year-old niece Sydney, who died by suicide in the fall of 2020. She believed in the power of youth to help one another learn how to be proactive in taking care of our mental health.

Sydney was brilliant and she had big goals. Her sophomore year of high school she created a proposal for a program called "Senti-Mental" as a school project with the goal of educating youth about mental health. Her big idea was to "break the stigma" of mental illness by educating students in the classroom about mental health. I hope this book will honor her life, and her dream of helping youth who are struggling with anxiety, depression, and thoughts of suicide.

I invite you to help make Sydney's dream of mental health education and resources for all children and youth come true. You can help end the stigma by breaking the silence about mental illness. You can also honor her life by being accepting of all people, no matter who they are or where they are on life's journey. By celebrating human diversity of gender, age, sexual orientation, race, culture, religion, nationality, and ability, we are creating welcoming, inclusive, supportive, and engaged communities, which are good for our mental health.

Thank you for being part of the solution and for joining the global movement for youth mental health justice. Together we can provide mental health education, resources, and support to children and teens everywhere. Together we can share hope and healing.

What You Will Find Inside:

1. A Love Letter to You from Your Blessed Mind
2. Pick Three Safeties
3. Take the Safety Pledge
4. Mental Health Crisis Resources—and space to build your own list of mental health resources
5. Self-Care While Helping a Friend
6. YCARE: A Tool to Help Others in a Mental Health Crisis
7. Prompts for Expressing How You Feel
8. Info on Depression, Anxiety, Therapy, and Medication
9. Tools for School
10. Things to Remember
11. A Letter of Hope

How To Use This Guide: If you're feeling down now and need help, start with 1-3. If you are not in crisis and want to collect resources for times when you may need them, start with 4. If you have a friend in need, look at 5-6.

A Love Letter to You from Your Blessed Mind

Dear Blessed Youth,

You are not broken. You are not bad. You are good. You are whole. You are loved.

Sometimes it feels like something is broken inside you. Sometimes it feels bad. This is not your fault. I need you to know that we are going to make things better.

To do that, I'm going to need your help.

First, talk to other people about what's going on inside your head. Choose three adults you trust and tell them what's going on inside your mind. Do it even if the thought of doing so is scary and even if you are nervous about what people will think. Even if you are worried you'll disappoint them, it's important to talk to adults you trust. It's more likely they'll be proud and relieved you said something. If the adult you chose to share with responds with anything other than love and support, please go on to the next adult. If someone is disappointed in you or blames you for the way you feel, they don't understand enough about mental health to be helpful. Please don't stop with them; find another adult to talk with.

Second, after you've told three adults, then ask for help. Tell them you need help figuring out what is going on inside your mind. Tell them you want to see a counselor. Tell them you want to see a doctor.

Third, talk to your teachers about including mental health education as part of the school day. Ask your teachers for mental health and brain breaks and for resources for mental health at school.

Fourth, try your best that if you are thinking of self-harm or suicide that you will tell someone and call 988 or 1-800-273-8255 or text the suicide helpline. Try your best.

I love you. I want you to love me back. We are truly awesome together. I know there are some things that are really hard right now.

We are in this together. We will grow through this, and we will be stronger, braver, and wiser for it. The mind is a brilliant part of you and so many creative people have minds that are different. We need people like you in the world.

You are not alone. You are part of this movement to share love and healing. We will get through this together.

Love,

Your Blessed Mind

P.S. *No matter what, you are loved! Stay. We need you. Try your best.*

Pick Three Safeties (3S)

Pick three people who are your "safeties." These are three adults in your life whom you promise to tell if you are thinking about self-harm. Let them know that they are one of your special people you are promising to contact if/when you are thinking of self-harm or suicide. These people could be a teacher, neighbor, friend's parent, minister, coach, nurse, doctor, parent, grandparent, aunt/uncle, youth director, Sunday school teacher or other adult relative.

Write down the names and phone numbers of your Three Safeties (3S):

1.

2.

3.

Take The Safety Pledge

Pledge to yourself that you will contact all three of these people (3S) when you begin having feelings or thoughts of self-harm and/or suicide.

I, ____________________, promise that when I start to have feelings or thoughts of self-harm and/or suicide, I will reach out immediately and contact my Three Safeties (3S). I promise that if I feel I am in crisis, I will call or text the suicide crisis line at 988 or 1-800-273-TALK (8255).

Sign your name here ________________________________

Date ________________________________

Witness ________________________________

Date ________________________________

Wear your Safety Pledge Safety Pin

As a conversation starter and a reminder of your promise, wear a safety pin with three beads on it, each bead representing a person you promise to tell when you begin to have feelings or thoughts of self-harm. You can make the Safety Pledge Pin on your own, with family and friends, at school or as part of a youth group activity to help break the silence, end the stigma and shame of mental illness. Wear your Safety Pledge Safety Pin and you just might help save a life, even if it is your own.

Mental Health Crisis Resources

National Suicide Prevention Lifeline: Call 988 or 1-800-273-TALK (8255) suicidepreventionlifeline.org

The Trevor Lifeline (specifically focused on suicide prevention for LGBTQ youth): 1-866-488-7386 thetrevorproject.org/get-help-now

Trevor Lifeline Text/Chat Services, available 24/7 Text "TREVOR" to 678-678

Crisis Text Line: Text TALK to 741-741 crisistextline.org

Build Your Own List of Mental Health Resources

When you get a chance (and when you're not in a crisis), talk with your parent or a teacher or a counselor about how to find mental health support in your own community.

- School counselors can often talk you through problems. They can also refer you for help.

  Your counselor's name and contact info: ____________

  ____

  ____

- Your school district may have a Student Support Services office with free or low-cost mental health help you can access. Here is a link to an example: https://www.sanjuan.edu/gethelp

What mental health supports does your district offer? List them here.

____

____

____

____

- Google "mental health resources for teens" and the name of your city or county. County public health services may offer care for free or at low cost. Or you may find another organization that offers care.

What resources are available through your county or independent groups (faith-based organizations, LGBTQ centers, university centers)?

____

____

____

____

Have a conversation with a family member to learn about resources you can access through health insurance or Medicaid. How can you use your family's health plan to access counseling or therapy?

____

____

____

____

Self-Care While Helping a Friend[1]

1. Even if you do give your best to support a friend who is struggling with their mental health, you can't control the choices they make. You are not responsible for anyone who dies by suicide.

2. Your feelings are important too. Mental health matters can be difficult and scary to talk about. It is a great idea for you to reach out for support from a trusted adult or counselor while helping a friend.

3. Practicing self-care is important for everyone. You may have a lot on your plate, from schoolwork to extracurricular activities to part-time job to relationships. Make sure to check in with your own physical, emotional, and mental health on a regular basis. It's ok to let the people you care about know when you are feeling overwhelmed and need support or a break.

4. You don't have to help someone all by yourself. Remember, you are empowering a friend to connect to resources and a trusted adult. If you are worried for your friend's life, it is ok to call 911 or the crisis hotline number 988 or 1-800-273-8255.

5. If a friend discloses that they are thinking of suicide and asks you not to tell anyone, this is not a secret you should keep. It is important that you let a trusted adult know that your friend is at risk for suicide; you should not carry this burden on your own. It is better to have your friend alive and mad at you than have them die by suicide.

---

[1] *Teaching Youth: Self-Care While Helping a Friend*, The Trevor Project, PDF File, accessed on November 22, 2021, https://www.thetrevorproject.org/wp-content/uploads/2017/09/Helping-Friend.pdf.

Y CARE: A Tool to Help Others in a Mental Health Crisis[2]

Y **Y**ou are never alone. It is not your fault when someone else dies by suicide. As friends, family, and loved ones, you can listen, support, and assist the person to get the help they need.

C **C**onnect the person to resources and to a supportive, trusted adult.

A **A**ccept and listen to the person's feelings and take them seriously.

R **R**espond if the person has a plan for suicide and tell someone you trust.

E **E**mpower the person to get help and to call a crisis line.

---

[2]*Lights, Camera, Empathy*, The Trevor Project, PDF File, accessed on November 22, 2021, https://www.thetrevorproject.org/wp-content/uploads/2017/09/Script-Writing.pdf.

Expressing How You Feel and Making the Body-Mind Connection

Doodle a Picture of Your Body

— What colors do you feel in your body?

— Where does it hurt?

— Where do you feel emotions like anger? Sadness? Anxiety? Confusion?

— What shapes or patterns do you feel or see in your body?

— Draw or write about how your body is feeling.

Doodle a Picture of Your Mind

— What colors do you feel in your mind?

— Which parts of your head or brain feel pain?

— What shapes or textures or patterns connect to how your mind feels?

— Draw or write about how your mind is feeling.

Doodle a Picture of Your Anxiety

— What shapes, textures, and colors are your anxiety?

— Where do you feel anxiety in your body?

— If your anxiety took the form of an animal, which animal would it be?

Doodle a Picture of Your Depression

— What shapes, textures, and colors are your depression?

— Where do you feel depression in your body?

— If your depression took the form of an animal, which animal would it be?

Doodle a Picture of Your Protections from Self-Harm

— What are some ways you can protect your body from thoughts of self-harm?

— Draw what that protection looks, sounds, smells, or feels like.

— Draw one thing you can do that is good for your body.

Doodle a Picture of Your Story

- What happened to you when you were a baby?
- What happened to you when you were a small child?
- What happened to you as you grew older?
- Draw a picture or write a story about what it was like for you growing up.

Doodle a Picture of Your Blessed Future

- What part of your story is waiting to be told?
- Who do you dream of becoming?
- Think about sharing this story with your Three Safeties (3S)

Your Brain and Body Are One

Part of what it means to be such an amazing, beautiful, complex, and beloved human being is that our brains make us this way. Our brains are amazing, beautiful, complex, and beloved parts of what makes us human. A lot goes on in our brains.

Our brains are blessed. We are who we are because of our brains. Some people call this self-aware part of us our mind. Our mind, and our physical brain, is the place where all our thoughts, feelings, emotions, and actions connect. Our emotions and our mental health impact how we think, feel, talk, act, learn, relate to others, and dream. We are one of the most complex species in the universe because of our amazing brains.

The human brain is where our mental health begins, but our mental health also extends throughout our bodies. Mental health affects our heart, our lungs, our stomach, our ears, our legs, our arms, and our sexual feelings and body parts.

Taking care of our brains includes getting enough sleep, eating healthy foods, getting exercise, drinking enough water, and making meaningful connections with others.

Mental health is connected to everything. With common childhood illnesses such as a cold, sinus infection, and the flu, there are symptoms we can measure, like checking to see if we have a fever or runny nose or cough or sore throat. But with mental illness, it's not always that simple.

A Story of My Brain and My Body

When I was in elementary school, I often had stomachaches. It wasn't because I was hungry or had eaten something bad. It was just this feeling deep inside that really hurt. My mom took me to the doctor, and they couldn't find anything wrong with me. I also had a problem sometimes wetting the bed.

This was so embarrassing. It turns out my body was trying to tell me something that my brain could not. I was stressed out.

My body was giving me signs that something was wrong in my brain. It was overwhelmed. The problems of my parents' divorce, my dad's mental illness, and my oldest brother Scott's mental illness where too much for my brain, and my body felt the effects. I was sensitive to all the chaos in my family, and it literally made me sick in my body. This is one example of the powerful body-mind connection we each have and how important it is to pay close attention to how your body feels. Your brain and body are super smart.

Depression and Anxiety Are Common. You are Not Alone

The most common types of mental illness for children and youth are depression and anxiety. Many people have both. That's true in my family. We all feel anxious and depressed some of the time. It is important to talk to a doctor to help you figure out if you have depression or anxiety. A doctor or therapist or psychiatrist will ask you about patterns in your emotions and feelings. What makes you feel worse, and what makes you feel better? The good news is there is a lot these professionals can do to help.

There is no shame in having depression and anxiety. You are not broken. There's just something going on inside your brain that needs extra attention. You are not defined by your diagnosis. You are a whole person who is an amazing part of the universe.

Am I Just Anxious or Is It Anxiety?

Everyone gets nervous, worried, or anxious. Right before taking a test or giving a speech or meeting new people, we can all feel a little overwhelmed. Our hearts race, our hands become sweaty, our breathing changes, and we feel as if we have to keep using the bathroom. This is all common and happens to everyone.

Anxiety is when these feelings are there most of the time and are too intense to ignore. When you cannot stop worrying and the worries keep you from getting good sleep, making friends, or focusing on school, then worries can turn into anxiety. It's good to know this about yourself. This knowledge is power. Our bodies tell us when something is wrong.

Anxiety becomes a mental health challenge when it becomes too much to handle, when you feel too much fear, nervousness, worry, or dread. Getting better can mean learning strategies to calm these feelings. Getter better can also mean getting support from a mental health professional who can help you through therapy and/or medication. Several people in my family really benefit from therapy and medication to treat anxiety. We've accepted this as part of our lives. We know that if we want to feel better, then we need to take these extra steps.

- **Generalized anxiety.** With this common anxiety disorder, a person worries excessively about many things. Someone with generalized anxiety may worry excessively about school, the health or safety of family members, and the future. They may always think of the worst that could happen. Along with the worry and dread, people with generalized anxiety have physical symptoms, such as chest pain, headache, tiredness, tight muscles, stomachaches, or vomiting. Generalized anxiety can lead a person to miss school or avoid social activities. With generalized anxiety, worries can feel like a burden, making life feel overwhelming or out of control.
- **Obsessive compulsive disorder (OCD).** For a person with OCD, anxiety takes the form of obsessions (thoughts) and compulsions (actions that try to relieve

anxiety). For example, what may start out as a healthy practice of handwashing becomes handwashing every few minutes.

- **Phobias.** These are intense fears of specific situations or things that are not actually dangerous, such as heights, dogs, or flying in an airplane. Phobias usually cause people to avoid the things of which they are afraid.
- **Social phobia (social anxiety).** Social situations or speaking in front of others trigger this intense anxiety. An extreme form called **selective mutism** causes some kids and teens to be too fearful to talk at all in certain situations.
- **Panic attacks.** These episodes of anxiety can occur for no apparent reason. With a panic attack, a person has sudden and intense physical symptoms that can include a pounding heart, shortness of breath, dizziness, numbness, or tingling feelings caused by overactivity of the body's normal fear response. **Agoraphobia** is an intense fear of panic attacks that causes a person to avoid going anywhere a panic attack could possibly occur.
- **Post-traumatic stress disorder (PTSD).** This type of anxiety disorder results from a traumatic or terrifying past experience. Symptoms include flashbacks, nightmares, or constant fear after the fact.

What Should I Do If I Have Anxiety?

Do you think you might have anxiety? Lots of people do and it is good to be honest with yourself. The good news is that there are treatments that will help you feel better, more relaxed, and more open to the good things in life. Treatment is not a cure. You might need to take special care of your mental health for most of your life. Working with a mental health professional to treat anxiety gives you the power back.

If you think you might have anxiety, here are four things you can do:

1. **Tell a parent or other adult about your physical sensations, worries, or fears.** Because anxiety disorders don't go away on their own, it's important to tell an adult who can help. If a parent doesn't seem to understand right away, talk to a school counselor, religious leader, or other trusted adult. This first step can be hard if you feel ashamed, embarrassed, or afraid of being judged. Know that I am so proud of you for telling someone. This is big. You are being brave. I know you can do it!

2. **Get a checkup.** Just like we see a doctor if we have a bad sore throat and fever, we also can see a doctor for other kinds of pain, whether physical or mental. Ask to see a doctor. One of my friends calls this a "check up from the neck up." Doctors can check whether you might have a physical condition that is causing the problems. For example, if you have stomach pain often or problems with going to the bathroom a lot, it could be anxiety related, or there may be something else happening with your body, such as a food allergy.

3. **Work with a mental health professional.** One of the best ways to alleviate anxiety is through talk therapy. Ask a doctor, nurse, or school counselor for a referral to someone who treats anxiety. In talk therapy you can find out what is causing your anxiety, and you'll figure out ways to feel better. Most of all, you will have a person you trust, to whom you can talk openly about everything, and who will support you no matter what. I love therapy because you can say whatever you need to say, get everything off your chest, and feel so much better. No one needs to hold everything inside all the time. We all need a safe space to cry, or scream, or just ask questions

without being judged. My friend calls this person who helps with mental health her "feelings doctor."

4. **Sleep, get regular exercise, and eat healthy foods.** Make sure you have a safe and comfortable place to sleep every night. Getting enough good sleep is one of the most important things you can do for your mental health. Moving your body and putting nutritious foods in your body are important tasks, too. Your brain needs sleep, exercise, and healthy foods.

Most of all, know how proud I am of you. You are brave. You are strong. You are courageous. I believe in you. You will feel better as you take these positive steps to support your mental health. Yay you!

Is it Just the Blues or Depression?

Everyone gets the blues. This is what happens when we feel sad and don't want to do anything. Sometimes we just want to stay in bed and not talk to anyone. Sometimes we cry. Sometimes we want to scream. Life can be too much sometimes. Feeling blue might last a day or two. If something sad happens, like the death of a pet or family member or friend, we can feel sad for a long time.

Depression is different from the blues. The blues will go away, and you'll start to feel like yourself again. But depression doesn't let go of you. Depression seems to want to stay for a long time, like weeks and months. If the blues are hanging on and keep dragging you down, it is important to talk to an adult and to seek the medical help of a doctor. The good news is that depression is a mental health diagnosis with lots of ways to get better. You can see a therapist, take medicine, and get extra supports so that you will feel good about yourself.

For a long time I thought that I was simply a sad person. I embraced this way of seeing the world. I thought that feeling sad was just the way I was made. Later, I realized that my long-term sadness was really depression. I wish I had gotten help for depression when I was a youth. I only started getting help as an adult, and being in therapy has really helped me a lot. I feel so much better. I still feel sad sometimes, but it is more manageable with the support of therapy.

When Sadness is Depression

When you're in a sad mood, it can seem as if it will last forever. But usually, feelings of sadness don't last very long—a few moments, a few hours, or maybe a day or two.

Sometimes sad feelings go on for too long, hurt too deeply, and make it hard to enjoy the good things about life. This deeper sadness that lasts a lot longer is called depression.

Depression can make problems seem too big to handle. When you are depressed, you might think things will never get better. You might feel as if you are worthless or bad. You may be sad or grumpy for weeks, or even longer. Sometimes depression may make you feel nothing, numb, and as if part of you is dead. You might even start not to feel hungry or enjoy the tastes or smells of food. Depression may make you not want to hang out with anyone anymore or feel too tired to do things like play, go to school, or go to work. Depression takes the joy out of life.

People get depressed for lots of reasons. Life is hard. When there are many bad or stressful things happening at once, that can cause depression. Sometimes depression can also run in families, like mine, and so you could be more likely to get it. Sort of like red hair or brown eyes. If you have depression, it is not your fault. And your life won't always be this hard and sad. Like anxiety, depression can be treated with mental health support and help.

How Do I Know If I Have Depression?[3]

- You constantly feel irritable, sad, or angry.
- Nothing seems fun anymore—even the activities you used to love—and you just don't see the point of forcing yourself to do them.
- You feel bad about yourself—worthless, guilty, or just "wrong" in some way.
- You sleep too much or not enough.
- You've turned to alcohol or drugs to try to change the way you feel.
- You have frequent, unexplained headaches or other physical pains or problems.
- Anything and everything makes you cry.
- You're extremely sensitive to criticism.
- You've gained or lost weight without consciously trying to do so.
- You're having trouble concentrating, thinking straight, or remembering things. Your grades or job performance may be plummeting because of it.
- You feel helpless and hopeless.
- You're thinking about death or suicide. (If so, talk to someone right away!) You can call the crisis hotline at 988 or 1-800-273-8255.

---

[3]"Dealing With Teen Depression," Help Guide, https://www.helpguide.org/articles/depression/teenagers-guide-to-depression.htm.

Getting Help for Depression, and Helping Yourself[4]

1. Let someone you trust know how you feel.
2. Reach out for help from a doctor or counselor who knows all about depression.
3. Take steps to live a happier life through therapy or medicine.
4. Make positive and simple changes such as:
   - Eat healthy foods
   - Get sufficient sleep
   - Walk, play, or find another way to exercise every day
   - Take time to relax
   - Take time to pray
   - Take time to notice the good things about life, no matter how small
   - Journal about your feelings
   - Talk to a friend about the good, the bad, the ugly, and the beautiful

What to Do If You Are Thinking About Self-Harm or Dying

In my family, sometimes depression can lead to thoughts of self-harm. This is hard to bear. If you have thoughts of self-harm, you are not alone and you are not a bad person. These thoughts are your mind's way of asking for help. Thoughts of self-harm come from a place of pain. As soon as you begin

[4] "What to Do When You Feel Sad," KidsHealth, last reviewed September 2021, https://kidshealth.org/en/kids/depression.html#catemotion.

to have thoughts of self-harm, tell a trusted adult right away.

Self-harm is tricky. It tricks your mind into thinking there's no way out and that nothing will ever change or get better. That's a big old lie. Self-harm is not your friend. Self-harm is the bully in your head. You need to get that under control as soon as possible. You don't want the self-harm bully to beat you up. This is why you'll need some help. Feeling depressed is not your fault. You are loved and you are not alone.

Thoughts of self-harm are a medical emergency.

Get help right away.

Self-harm can lead to death by suicide.

I am feeling suicidal, what do I do?

If this is you, tell someone how you feel.

Contact your Three Safeties (3S).

Ask an adult for help.

Visit a suicide help site, like the National Suicide Prevention Lifeline, or call their helpline at 988 or 1-800-273-TALK (8255).

Call 911.

Go to an emergency room.

Reach out for the help you deserve.

People on lifelines, helplines, and at emergency rooms are trained to help you feel better.

You will be ok.

This terrible feeling will not last forever.

Stay.

We want you to live.

You are loved.

Say this out loud, "I am loved. I will do my best to stay."

One Youth's Story About Self-Harm and Calling 911[5]

This is the story of someone who felt like harming themselves and called 911.

(calls 911): *"My name is Kim and I'm not feeling safe. I am having thoughts of hurting myself. I need help. My address is 123 Rainbow Road. I have a plan for suicide, but I am scared."*

911 Operator: "You did the right thing by calling. Stay on the phone with me and I'm sending someone out to you right now. It will take a few minutes, but someone is one their way to help you. Just stay on the phone."

"ok. I am really upset (crying). I don't know what is happening."

"You are going to be ok. We are going to keep you safe. Is anyone else in the house with you?"

"No. I am alone."

"ok, someone is on their way now."

"ok."

"Did you go to school today?"

"No, I stayed home sick."

"Where are your parents?"

"I just live with my mom and she's at work."

"What is your mom's name and where does she work?"

DING DONG—the doorbell rings—

"That's the door."

"ok, that's the emergency response team. They are here to help you."

---

[5]Real-life episode shared with permission. Personal details changed to protect privacy.

Every situation is different. When you call 911, it's important to share that you or your loved one is having a mental health emergency. Ask for a trained Crisis Intervention Team or someone trained to help people in a mental health crisis. Depending on the situation, the emergency responder may stay with the person until someone else returns home, then talk with a caregiver about next steps. If the person experiencing an emergency is an adult and does not have a caregiver, the team will try to de-escalate the crisis and help the person feel more stable. Then the emergency responders can help connect the person with a care provider or get them to an emergency psychiatric facility.

Mental Health Survival With Therapy

I dream about a world where every child and teen have a mental health therapist. A therapist is a person trained to work with you and your brain as you develop and grow. Talk therapy entails meeting with a person who listens to us and asks questions about our life. Therapists help us find healthy ways to cope with stress and difficult problems, make big decisions, and find joy in life.

Most people only see a therapist after there's a big problem. Or their teacher makes them go talk to the school counselor because they've gotten in trouble. But this doesn't make sense to me. Mental health should be part of our preventive care system, and healthy brain development should be something our schools take care of proactively.

Sometimes your pediatrician or nurse will ask you about your home life and how things are going at school, or they will have other "screening" questions at your appointments to help them decide whether they should refer you for mental health care. This is good, but a lot of people stop going to the doctor for annual checkups at some point, or maybe we just go for a flu shot or a sports physical, or to get birth control, or when we have a weird rash. There's no one who is really invested in our healthy brain and mental development.

In my dream future all children and teens can see a counselor or therapist before there are any problems with their brain. Do you have a therapist? If not, now is the perfect time to get one. Ask your parents to schedule you for a meeting with a therapist and spend a session just talking with them about your life, your goals, and your happiness. Schedule a yearly checkup with them. That way, you'll have someone you already trust to turn to if you need regular therapy sessions to work on a specific problem.

With What Problems Do Therapists Help? What Happens in Therapy?[6]

Therapists are trained to help people with all kinds of problems: family, school, friends, bullying, or health problems. Therapists help people with painful feelings like sadness, anger, stress, worry, low self-esteem, and fear. Therapists help treat mental health conditions such as anxiety, depression, and self-harm. It's ok to try out more than one therapist. The first therapist may not be a good match for you. Don't give up. Seek out a therapist that is a good fit for you.

At first, your therapist will talk with you, ask questions, and listen to learn more about you. This helps your therapist understand the problem. Together you will make goals for the things for which you want help.

In therapy sessions, you might do the following:

- **Talk.** Therapists invite people to talk about their feelings. Talking is a healthy way to express feelings. It helps people feel accepted, understood, and ready to learn.

---

[6] "Going to a Therapist," KidsHealth, last reviewed November 2021, https://kidshealth.org/en/teens/therapist.html#catfeeling-sad.

- **Do activities.** Therapists might teach lessons about emotions, coping skills, or facing fears. Activities and worksheets or app-based exercises can help to make these lessons interesting.
- **Practice new skills.** A therapist might teach skills like mindfulness and calm breathing. You might learn ways to face fears, to lower stress, or how to speak up for yourself. In your therapy meetings, you might practice the skills you learn.
- **Solve problems.** Your therapist will ask how problems affect you at home and at school. You will talk together about how to solve these problems.

One Youth's Story About Getting Therapy[7]

Anthony can't remember the last time he went to the doctor. His mom has diabetes that is usually under control, but she goes to the ER any time she feels out of whack. He doesn't want her to take him to the ER for his mental health challenge. But Anthony does tell his aunt that he thinks he needs help.

She takes him to prayer group at church. The elderly women pray for Anthony. He feels silly being prayed over and he asks them not to "lay hands" on him. They respect his wishes. But they do pray out loud for him and tell him they love him. They make him feel like it is ok to feel the way he feels. He asks, "What does it mean that God will heal me?" His aunt says, "God will help you take the next step, whatever that is. We will help you too."

Anthony decides to ask his favorite teacher at school for help. Anthony's teacher helps him make an appointment with the school counselor. So he goes there. *This is a lot of steps, God*, he thinks. *What am I actually doing*? His mind goes blank

[7]A made-up story based on parts of different true ones combined. Personal details change to "fictional story" to protect privacy.

in the counselor's office. He tries to answer questions about himself but ends up leaving the office after about ten minutes of awkwardness.

Anthony spends the next day in bed. He checks his Google classroom and school email around 5 p.m. and sees a note from the counselor with a link to a TikTok account made by a community organization called Youth Help Network. The TikToks are cheesy, but Anthony doesn't hate them. The group has an Instagram account too, so he checks that. There are many encouraging messages on there. He learns about a meeting called Fellas With Feelings on Tuesday nights—*Haha,* he thinks. *No way am I ready to talk with a whole room of strangers about my feelings!* But, there's also a phone number. *Oh good, they respond to texts too.*

The next day Anthony calls the number after trying and "Ending Call" several times. He finally gets through and talks to someone. They help him figure out a script for talking to his mom about getting to the county health department—a special youth office not too far from his school—where he can meet with a therapist. His mom is grateful for the information. She doesn't yet understand what he needs, but she is happy to take him to get help.

Mental Health Survival With Medications

When our brains get sick, we give them medicine. Taking medicine for anxiety, depression, and other mental illnesses can help us feel better. Just as some people take medicine to lower their blood pressure or fever, we can take medicines to adjust our brain chemistry. There is nothing wrong or weak about taking medicine for one's mental health.

Many people in my family take medications for anxiety, depression, ADHD, and bipolar disorder. It's important to work closely with a doctor when beginning, adjusting, or stopping medications. Sometimes meds have bad side effects and need to be changed. Sometimes meds stop working. And sometimes meds don't work at all. Most of the time, doctors can help find the right medication that will help you feel better. It's common to treat anxiety and depression through a combination of talk therapy and medications.

One Family Story About Antidepressants

Don't be afraid of taking medicine for your brain. I learned a lot from my grandmother who lived to be ninety-nine years old. In her later life, she started going to painting classes and spent many Saturdays doing oil painting. She was healthy and lived alone even in her nineties. One day during one of my visits I saw her taking her medicine at breakfast.

She said, "I'm taking my little happy pill." When I asked her about it, she told me how her doctor had prescribed her an antidepressant. My grandma was one of the happiest people I have ever known. Yet even she needed some help. I figured if my grandma needed a little boost, then probably most of us at some point in our lives can be helped through mental health medicine. If you are worried about taking medicine, just think of my grandma. She is a great example of someone who is not ashamed of needing a little help to feel better. It turns out lots of people in my family take antidepressants!

If you are taking mental health medications and they are making you feel worse, tell someone right away. This happened to a person in my family when their anti-anxiety medicine was causing thoughts of self-harm, a very dangerous side effect. Thankfully we told the doctor, who helped change the medication. Medicines are meant to help us feel better. Pay attention to how medications are making you feel.

Lots of children and teens take medicine for their mental health. Medicine, along with talk therapy, and family support, is an important resource for our mental health survival.

Mental Health Survival Tools for School

Your knowledge is power! The more you know, the more you can change yourself and the world for the better. Once you've begun to take better care of your own mental health, then you can begin to help others get mental health support. Start with the people with whom you spend the most time—probably your family, friends, and people at school.

One of the most powerful ways you can make a difference in the world (after first taking care of yourself) is to use your power to help your school take mental health seriously. You can talk to the teachers and the administrators of your school about how mental health education in school is just as important as math, science, English, and history. By teaching about mental health now, we can help people before they get into a mental health crisis.

My niece Sydney was a big believer in bringing mental health education into the schools. She said that this would help empower youth to ask for help and to make the shame and stigma of mental illness go away. Talking about anxiety, depression, and self-harm in school lets kids know what to look out for and how to get resources for support. When you raise your voice about important issues like mental health, you are using your power in a positive way to help others. This is called advocacy.

Advocacy is how we work together to make things better. Each one of us has a voice and power that we can use to create positive change. Advocacy is one way we can do the work of mental health justice, so that everyone gets mental health resources and support. Schools are an excellent place for this to happen.

You can talk to student groups on campus, student leaders, and also the school board. The mayor of your city would probably also like to know, even the governor of your state. If you want, you can even write a letter to the President of the United States telling her what you are doing for mental health. (Someday we will have a woman president, I just know it!)

The key when working with your school is to find a "champion," someone who will help you and work together with you. This effort will take time, patience, and a team. Reach out to national groups such as the Trevor Project and Sandy Hook Promise and see what resources they have to support your efforts. *WE* are in this together! Together, we can make a difference, helping people, sharing hope, and saving lives!

Your Life, Your Voice, Your Power

Let's say you've decided, "yes! I'm going to speak out!" That's fantastic. So—what, exactly, should you speak out about? What solutions might be a good fit for the mental health challenges kids are dealing with at your school? Here are a few ideas.

Advocate for Student Mini-Brain Breaks, which are shown to significantly reduce stress levels in children and youth. For more information and examples of how other students have done this, see UNICEF USA Kid Power program.[8]

Advocate for daily mental health screenings. For your school, this might mean every student checking in at the beginning of class with a thumb up, sideways or down. Or it might look like holding up a color coded piece of paper with green for good, yellow for ok, and red for needing extra help.

Advocate for Suicide Prevention Education. See the example letter on p. 45 (Please Bring Suicide Prevention Education to Our School).

Advocate for your school to create peer support groups. Get started by learning whether any neighboring schools have a

---

[8]Unicef Kid Power, https://www.unicefkidpower.org/brain-breaks-for-kids/

peer support group. If so, learn how their group works, how it got started, and the projects or accomplishments of which they're most proud. If there are no similar groups in your area, check out organizations like National Alliance on Mental Illness (NAMI), which has an On Campus Club network through their state affiliates with tools to help you get a club started at your school.

Advocate for in-school mental health counselors. Get started by asking a teacher what it would take to create a schoolwide policy allowing students to visit a counselor or nurse for reasons other than physical illness, or to have a hall pass for reasons other than bathroom emergencies. See the sample Hall Pass on p. 44.

Advocate for in-school mental health education (mental health first aid). For more information and examples of how other schools have done this, look up on the internet Mental Health First Aid.[9]

Mental Health Hall Pass/Nurse's Pass:

This is an example hall pass you can create to support the school advocacy steps described above. After getting agreement from Student Leadership, the PTA, and/or your school administration on how the passes may be used, you can then encourage teachers to include several copies of this form when they hand out class orientation material at the beginning of the semester, or any time there are papers to hand back to students. That way, students will have the pass available to them in their binders. When they feel bad and cannot concentrate in class, they can circle one or more of the following phrases to show their teacher and be excused.

---

[9] "Mental Health First Aid for Schools," Mental Health First Aid, https://www.mentalhealthfirstaid.org/population-focused-modules/schools/.

I'm not okay

I feel alone

I feel disconnected

I feel confused

I feel scared

I feel lost

I feel down

I feel depressed

I feel anxious

I feel angry

I feel hopeless

I feel like dying

My head hurts

My stomach hurts

My body hurts

(Your write one:) ______________________________

HALL PASS

The hall pass gives you permission to take care of your mental health. It can say:

I need to go:

see my counselor

To the office

Call home

Other__________

Please Bring Suicide Prevention Education to [School Name]![10]

[First Name, Last Name] [Title]

[Name of School] [Street Address]

[City, State, Zip]

Dear [Mr./Mrs./Ms./Mx.] [Last Name],

I am writing to ask you to bring suicide prevention education to [name of school]. As a student of [name of school], I care deeply about the health and safety of my friends and classmates.

Suicide is the second leading cause of death among youth aged ten through twenty-four. And my peers who are lesbian, gay, or bisexual are four times more likely to attempt suicide than my straight peers.

These statistics are staggering, but with your support we can take action. Suicide is preventable!

The Trevor Lifeguard Workshop, offered by The Trevor Project, is a free training program that can be used by teachers and school counselors in classrooms. The fifteen-minute video and accompanying materials of the Trevor Lifeguard Workshop are listed in the SPRC/AFSP Best Practices Registry for Suicide Prevention and provide students in grades six through twelve with real tools and information about how they can help themselves and others who may be in crisis or thinking about suicide. You can learn more by visiting http://www.TheTrevorProject.org/Lifeguard.

Let's join thousands of schools across the country by offering Trevor Lifeguard Workshops to the students of [name of school]. Together we can help save lives.

Sincerely,

[Name]

---

[10] The Trevor Project, https://www.thetrevorproject.org/education/lifeguard-workshop/.

Things to Remember

You are amazing.

You are beautiful.

You are complex (in a good way).

You are a beloved human being.

Your brain is different and good.

The fact that you exist is a miracle and a dream come true.

You are here for a reason.

You may not know your reason yet, but trust me, it is a really good one.

Your life is important.

Getting better takes time.

Be patient and gentle with yourself.

You are more than your disability, disease, illness, or diagnosis.

It's ok to be different.

It's ok not to be ok for a while.

Your life matters to me.

Try your best.

Breathe.

Stay.

A Letter of Hope[11]

dear stranger,

almost one year on antidepressants. there's a lot to think about. i came out. i joined my catholic school's lgbt group. started volunteering at a lgbt center. got my driving permit. started my first job. applied to scholarships, graduated from high school summa cum laude, was accepted to my dream school. celebrated my anniversary with my girlfriend. in all honesty, i am proud of what i've accomplished.

but i still have depression and anxiety. sure, i've learned to manage it better, i'm out of a long-lasting and deep rut, and my worst days are less frequent. but I still have days, weeks, when i see no point of getting out of bed or talking to anybody. my brain tells me i have no friends. i hear echoes sometimes when my head seems empty. what if i get worse again? what if the meds are the only thing keeping me somewhat sane?

so what? ups and downs are natural in life. and there's nothing wrong with needing a little help. so what? i'm managing each day, and that's what matters. what matters is that i'm alive, i've made strides, and i'm learning more about who i am every day. i'm still teaching myself that i am enough. i can see a light at the end of the tunnel, and i know each day is another chance for happiness. i'll be damned if i don't give each chance my best shot.

yours truly,

a stranger

---

[11]Reprinted with permission from Letters to Strangers. *A Youth-for-Youth Mental Health* Guidebook (Morrisville, NC: LuLu Press, 2019).

Mental Health Crisis and Support

- National Suicide Prevention Lifeline: Call 988 or 1-800-273-TALK (8255) suicidepreventionlifeline.org
- The Trevor Lifeline (specifically focused on suicide prevention for LGBTQ youth): 1-866-488-7386 thetrevorproject.org/get-help-now
- Trevor Lifeline Text/Chat Services, available 24/7 Text "TREVOR" to 678-678
- Crisis Text Line: Text TALK to 741-741 crisistextline.org

Mental Health Organizations

- American Foundation for Suicide Prevention: www.afsp.org
- Child Mind Institute: www.childmind.org
- National Alliance on Mental Illness: www.nami.org
- Mental Health America: www.mentalhealthamerica.org
- Mental Health First Aid: www.mentalhealthfirstaid.org
- Pathways to Promise: www.pathways2promise.org
- Trevor Project: www.trevorproject.org
- United Church of Christ Mental Health Network: www.mhn-ucc.org
- Youth For Youth Mental Health Guidebook: www.letterstostrangers.org

If someone's life is in danger, call 911 or your local emergency number.

Additional crisis support services for specific needs:

- **Child Sexual Abuse.** Stop It Now! Phone: 1-888-PREVENT (1-888-773-8368)
- **Crime Victims.** National Center for Victims of Crime. Phone: 1-855-4VICTIM (1-855-484-2846)
- **Dating Abuse.** Love is Respect. Phone: 1-866-331-9474, TTY: 1-866-331-8453, or Text LOVEIS TO 22522
- **Disaster Distress.** SAMHSA Disaster Distress Helpline. Phone or Text: 1-800-985-5990
- **Domestic Violence.** National Domestic Violence Hotline. Phone: 1-800-799-SAFE (1-800-799-7233), TTY: 1-800-787-3224
- **Missing and Abducted Children.** Child Find of America, Inc. Phone: 1-800-I-AM-LOST (1-800-426-5678), or National Center for Missing & Exploited Children. Phone: 1-800-THE-LOST (1-800-843-5678)
- **Rape and Sexual Abuse.** Rape, Abuse & Incest National Network. Phone: 1-800-656-HOPE (1-800-656-4673)
- **Runaway and Homeless Youth.** National Runaway Safeline. Phone: 1-800-RUNAWAY (1-800-786-2929), or Text: 66008